MORE RAVE REVIEWS

"A delightfully illustrated, inclusive guide to help kids evaluate their behavior, tune into their feelings, figure out how to start a conversation, be a good listener, and interact in simple and emotionally charged situations."

— **CHRISTINE KOH,** coauthor of *Minimalist Parenting*
and cohost of the *Edit Your Life* podcast

"An accessible primer on how to be more loving, inclusive, self-confident, and, indeed, a better human."

— **JENNY TRUE,** "Dear Jenny" columnist on Romper and
author of *You Look Tired: An Excruciatingly Honest Guide to New Parenthood*

"*What Can I Say?* reminds us how much interacting in a healthy way with those around us enriches our lives. From compromise to gratitude to forgiveness to compassion, Catherine Newman reminds youth and the adults who care about them of the importance of humanity in communication."

— **ABIGAIL GEWIRTZ,** author of *When the World Feels Like a Scary Place*
and editor-in-chief of the *International Journal of Psychology*

"One of the most important things adults can teach children is the skill of communication and self-advocacy. *What Can I Say?* can not only teach children to be more confident, eloquent, and clear, it can save them from harm and give them the tools and courage they need to ask for help."

— **JESSICA LAHEY,** *New York Times* best-selling
author of *The Gift of Failure* and *The Addiction Inoculation*

"Newman is out with another totally gorgeous guide for kids about how to succeed in the world. This book is to Gen Z what *Free to Be You and Me* was to Gen X. You'll find yourself wishing you'd had it years ago!"

— **JULIE LYTHCOTT-HAIMS,** *New York Times* best-selling
author of *How to Raise an Adult* and *Your Turn*

WHAT CAN I SAY?

A Kid's Guide to Super-Useful Social Skills to Help You Get Along and Express Yourself

CATHERINE NEWMAN
ILLUSTRATIONS BY DEBBIE FONG

Storey Publishing

The mission of Storey Publishing is to serve our customers by publishing practical information that encourages personal independence in harmony with the environment.

Edited by Deanna F. Cook and Mia Lumsden
Art direction and book design by Ash Austin
Text production by Jennifer Jepson Smith
Illustrations by © Debbie Fong

Storey books are available at special discounts when purchased in bulk for premiums and sales promotions as well as for fund-raising or educational use. Special editions or book excerpts can also be created to specification. For details, please call 800-827-8673, or send an email to sales@storey.com.

Storey Publishing
210 MASS MoCA Way
North Adams, MA 01247
storey.com

Printed in the United States by Versa Press
10 9 8 7 6 5 4 3 2 1

MADE
in the
USA

LIBRARY OF CONGRESS CATALOGING-IN-PUBLICATION DATA ON FILE

For my kids and my kids' friends and
my friends' kids and my nieces and nephews
and niblings, and for all the kids everywhere
who have shown me what it means to
communicate lovingly, gracefully,
hilariously, courageously, and with beautiful,
authentic awkwardness.
—Catherine

For all the kids who struggle (like I did) to
speak up for themselves and others.
—Debbie

CONTENTS

HOW TO BE YOUR BEST SELF

- - - - - - - - - - - - - - -

THE BASICS

This is a book about how to talk to the other people in your life (you can probably figure out how to talk to yourself on your own) because our relationships are what give our lives meaning! Relationships with our friends and family, for sure, but also with our neighbors and teachers, our teammates and classmates, our fellow citizens and crushes and pets. Okay, you already know what to say to your pets—**"Sit"** and **"Stay"** and **"Who's a good boy?"** and **"Which one of you ate my underpants?"** But that still leaves the humans: What do you say to them? And how? And, also, when?

It depends on the situation, of course! And this book tries to cover a lot of different situations: easier conversations and harder ones; in-person talking and the kind you might do over text or email. Other people's ways of being in the world can be so confusing.

But you already have the tools you need—empathy, curiosity, and care—to learn the skills you need to connect with other people, just like you've learned the skills of making a sandwich or cutting a heart out of a folded piece of paper. Skills that might take practice, sure, but that you can master over time so you can live happily and well in the world of people.

BUT WHY?

Learning how to be more kind, gracious, expressive, compassionate, responsible, respectful, and authentic in your interactions is going to make the world a better place, filled with happier people. Plus, it's going to help you in a million ways: Your friends might adore you more, your parents might agree to more stuff, your peers might be more likely to respect your opinions, your teachers might give you the benefit of the doubt, and maybe even strangers will fall all over themselves to help you.

Even if you experience conflicts and disappointments in your relationships sometimes (and you will), you'll know how to handle them better. If how you're acting and interacting feels right, so will everything else. Plus, as one of my own kids once said,

"YOU'RE NEVER GOING TO BE LYING ON YOUR DEATHBED WISHING YOU'D BEEN A BIGGER JERK."

There's not a single right way to be, though. You might be an introvert or an extrovert, shy, outgoing, or really just more into your pets than you are into people. "Normal" is not a thing, and everyone doesn't have to be the same kind of person.

You might even have extra challenges when it comes to interacting with other people. You might be on the autism spectrum, say, or experience social anxiety that makes small talk feel like you're waiting in line for a roller coaster you never even said you wanted to ride. That's fine. You can just be how you are—skipping what seems impossible for now but putting a mental or actual bookmark there in case anything changes and you feel that you'd like to try it out.

It's also okay to be noisy (or silent), to cry, to say no, to disturb people when you need to, to express yourself in a way that's different from how other people express themselves. Doing and saying the right thing is not always about smoothing the rough edges, conforming to norms, or making everybody's life easier.

Justice, for example, has never come about from people sitting politely with their pinky fingers extended away from their teacups chatting mildly about the weather. Will you make mistakes in your relationships and interactions? Of course! Will you learn from them? You will.

What matters most is that you try to be your best self and balance other people's needs with your own. What matters is that, more often than not, the question you ask out loud or in your own head is **"What can I do here to help?"** What matters is that you've spoken your truth and have also been respectful of other people's selves, of their intrinsic worth as human beings. It's a lot to ask, but we're asking it.

ALL
OF
US

We want this book to be as inclusive as possible. We're trying not to assume that everyone has or should have the same cognitive, neurological, or physical abilities. When we say "family," we're not picturing a particular family-shaped cookie cutter stamping out identical families; we know that there are so many different kinds of, um, family-shaped cookies, and you might live with one or two parents—and/or with different caregivers, including stepparents, foster parents, aunts, uncles, or grandparents.

And if there are parts of this book that don't work for you because of your own cultural background, religious beliefs, or family values, then you may need to try different strategies from the ones we suggest. Because people are different. (Thank goodness!)

If you notice ways this book could be more inclusive, in either its scope or its advice, please share by writing me at the contact page on my website, CatherineNewmanWriter.com. I'd be so grateful.

ARE YOU READY? ⟶
LET'S GET THIS CONVERSATION STARTED.

THE BEHAVIOR TEST

If you're ever stumped about how to act or what to say, we've come up with four ways to test the rightness of what you're doing or saying:

The Golden Rule Test

Is this what you would want someone else to do or say if you were on the other side of the situation? (This is a form of empathy!)

I KNOW THIS IS HARD, BUT I'M WITH YOU.

I'M SO GLAD YOU'RE HERE!

The Universal Test

Would the world be a better place if everyone acted this way?

The Regret Test
Are you going to wish you had acted or spoken differently? It can be hard to predict this in the moment, so just do your best.

The Authenticity Test
Is this what you think is right and true, on a gut level? Trust your instincts.

I DON'T THINK THAT STEREOTYPE IS FUNNY.

CHAPTER 1

HOW TO MEET, GREET & PART

Hi! Hello! It's nice to meet you! So long! Farewell! See you tomorrow! People come together and part company again all the time. We see people we know, and we meet people we didn't know before. Sometimes it might feel a little awkward, or even a *lot* awkward. But it's important, it's quick, and you can totally do it. (Hint: "It's nice to meet you, too.")

HOW TO
GREET SOMEONE

Why you say hi to someone is to acknowledge that you're in the same space, either actually or virtually—but *how* you do it depends a little bit on the context. In any case, you'll want to be friendly (of course) and make eye contact (although eye-contact expectations vary across cultures, plus this might not be something you can do without your skin crawling off of your body).

YOU'RE MEETING ANYONE

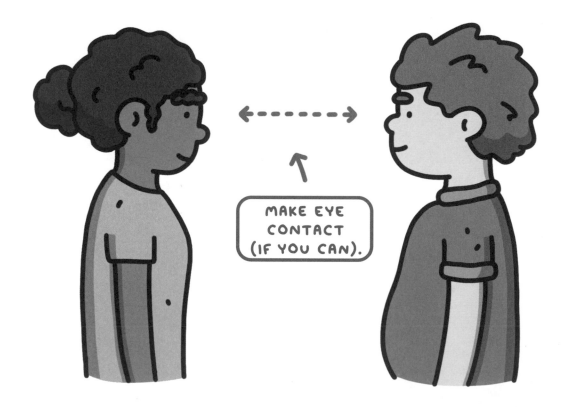

MAKE EYE
CONTACT
(IF YOU CAN).

YOU'RE MEETING A FRIEND TO PLAY FRISBEE

YOU RUN INTO SOMEONE YOU KIND OF KNOW AT THE DRUG STORE

YOUR FRIEND'S LITTLE BROTHER
ANSWERS THE DOOR

YOU'RE ON A
VIDEO CALL

YOUR GRANDMA
CALLS YOU

#AWKWARD

When you're approaching someone you know in the hallway or on the street, when do you start making eye contact and/or when do you say hi? (I didn't even ask if you weirdly pretend not to even see them!) There's no right answer. Everyone in my house finds this uniquely challenging for some reason.

HOW TO INTRODUCE YOURSELF

If you end up sitting next to someone you don't know or are paired with a new person in social studies, talking to a new friend's parents (or your parents' new friends), or meeting someone in any other way, it's friendly to introduce yourself.

EMAIL

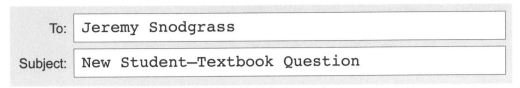

To: Jeremy Snodgrass

Subject: New Student—Textbook Question

Dear Mr. Snodgrass,

My name is Reiko, and I'm going to be in your math class this year. I had a question about the textbook . . .

PHONE

HI! MY NAME IS JASMINE JONES, AND I'M CALLING ABOUT THE BABYSITTING JOB.

JUST SAYING. If you're not sure you heard the person's name right or you're not sure you understand how to pronounce it, just ask them to repeat it, then say it back to make sure you got it. You don't need to act puzzled or laugh or act like they have a weird name. You just need to make a sincere effort to say their name the right way. (See page 140 to learn how to make gender-inclusive introductions.)

HOW TO
INTRODUCE
OTHER PEOPLE

If you end up in a situation with people you know who don't know *each other*, then introducing them will help make them feel comfortable and included. (Bonus points for giving them something to connect about.)

GRANDPA, THIS IS MY MATH TUTOR, PEARL. PEARL, THIS IS MY GRANDPA JOE, WHO HAD TO RELEARN LONG DIVISION FOUR TIMES, JUST LIKE ME!

HOW TO
PUT SOMEONE AT EASE

Someone might be feeling uncomfortable because they're new or nervous or shy, but you can help make them feel calm and relaxed just by being friendly.

Your kind, approachable vibe is the most important thing—and this is likely to include a warm smile.

MAYBE **TOO MUCH** SMILE, ACTUALLY?

PERFECT!

You can also say something to make them feel welcome or comfortable in a possibly awkward situation.

HOW TO
SAY GOODBYE

Concluding an interaction is like putting a period at the end of a sentence: *Done*. Say a friendly goodbye or offer a clear sign-off, and then everyone knows you're out. You don't want your friends to be like, "Wait, is Brian still here?" or have a teacher wonder if you hit *send* before your email was finished. (I know, I know. Nobody puts a period at the end of a text—it's a major exception.)

IN PERSON

SHUFFLE MY CARDS BACK INTO THE DECK! I GOTTA GO HOME FOR DINNER. THANK YOU SO MUCH FOR HAVING ME OVER.

ALSO IN PERSON

CARDS AND LETTERS

EMAIL

To:	Jocelyn Corncob
Subject:	School Mascot Tryouts

Dear Mrs. Corncob,

I'm interested in trying out to be one of our school's blobfish mascots. Would you please send me details about the audition?

Sincerely,
Angelina

NICE EMAIL SIGN-OFF, ANGELINA!

JUST SAYING. You might not feel comfortable with handshakes, hugs, or kisses, and that's fine. Whether or not to physically touch another person in greeting or parting is a decision everyone gets to make for themselves. "I'm not a hugger, but I'm so glad to see you!" you can say to someone who opens their arms in greeting.

Or you might prefer a little awkward wave or fist bump!

POP QUIZ!

There's a new kid on the block! She's around your age, and you see her tossing a ball by herself when you take your dog out for a walk. What do you do?

1 Pretend you don't see her and whistle loudly so she sees how busy you are whistling.

2 Turn around, dart back into your house, and fake a stomachache so your sister has to take the dog out.

3 Say, "Hi! You must be our new neighbor!" and introduce yourself—then ask if she'd like to play catch sometime.

4 Say, "Um, uh, hi, I'm, er, we're neighbors!"

Answer: 3 or 4. Any kind of greeting or welcome, even if you feel awkward about it, is friendlier than slinking past someone or running away.

CHAPTER 2

HOW TO HAVE A CONVERSATION

- - - - - - - - - - - - - - - - -

A conversation means talking, listening, and exchanging ideas with another person or a group of people. Sometimes, having a conversation can feel kind of tricky. But don't worry! We've got some helpful strategies to try if any of it ever seems kind of baffling to you.

HOW TO
EXPRESS CURIOSITY

Everyone who's not you is different from you! That (obvious) fact is at the heart of curiosity—and curiosity is at the heart of good conversation. You can express curiosity with deep questions, silly questions, or odd questions. Not coincidentally, the most interesting people are the people who are *most interested in other people*!

Stumped? Try one of these 10 curiosity sparks:

1 Would you rather be a squirrel preparing for the winter or a bear waking up from hibernation in the springtime?

2 What is one question you wish you absolutely 100 percent knew the answer to?

3 Would you rather be able to fly or be invisible?

4 What's something you're good at that most people don't know about you?

5 Potato chips in a sandwich: yes or no?

 6 What's something about how we live that kids a hundred years from now are going to think is really weird ?

7 Were you secretly scared of anything when you were little?

8 If you could have a third eye anywhere on your body, where would you put it?

 9 What's the best TV show you've ever seen in your life?

10 Do you think there's other intelligent life in the universe?

HOW TO LISTEN

Good listening means making a sincere effort to pay attention to another person's experience. Which is weirdly simple—but also weirdly challenging! People want to feel known and understood and like what they're saying matters. Here are some ways to help:

Get ready to listen. If somebody you care about is telling you something, prepare to pay attention. That might mean finishing what you're doing first, putting your phone away, or sitting down. If it's a bad time to talk because your cat just barfed a hairball onto the white carpet, say so, then suggest another time when you'll be available to listen.

OOPS.

Quiet your mind. This is very Zen advice, and it's kind of hard to describe. But it might mean taking some deep breaths so that you're focused on the conversation you're having instead of being distracted by, say, the homework you were just doing.

Show that you're listening. You can make sure you understand what the other person is saying by saying it back to them in your own words. Or you can use body language—nodding your head or making eye contact—to show them that you're following along.

Ask follow-up questions.
Some conversations evolve naturally: One person tells a story about their toilet catastrophically clogging, and it reminds you of the time a gigantic spider jumped out of your shower drain. But it can also be helpful to let someone finish their thought by asking them questions about it before you share your own story.

JUST SAYING. Sometimes people want to talk to us in a way that's, uh, less interesting than might be ideal (*boring*). What then? See if you can steer the conversation to a topic that's more compelling to both of you. Or try asking a deeper question: "I think I get the gist of how you play *Snoring Sloths*. Tell me three other things you like that aren't video games."

HOW TO
MAKE SMALL TALK

Sometimes you're not having a deep conversation; you're just filling a little time—or preventing the nightmare of awkward silence—by chitchatting about nothing in particular. This is called "small talk," and you might make it with the person next to you in chorus or with your frightening great aunt or while you're waiting for a video call to start.

Classic topic recommendations include the weather, favorite movies or shows, and hobbies. But small talk doesn't have to be boring! The curiosity sparks on page 34 can work just as well, and they might help you get to know someone better, too.

RIGHT

NICE WEATHER WE'RE HAVING, AUNTIE OPHELIA, AM I RIGHT?

IF YOU LIKE SUNSHINE, WHICH I DO NOT.

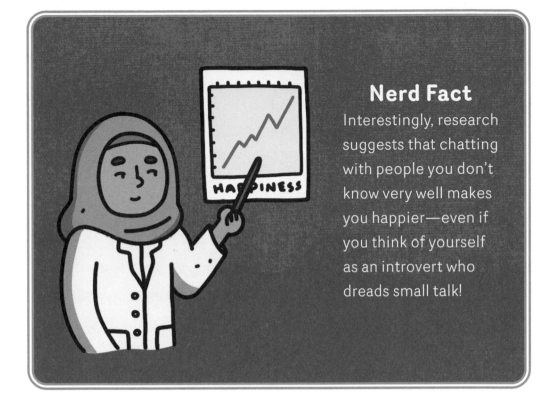

Nerd Fact

Interestingly, research suggests that chatting with people you don't know very well makes you happier—even if you think of yourself as an introvert who dreads small talk!

ALSO RIGHT

WOULD YOU EVER PUT POTATO CHIPS IN A TUNA SANDWICH?

DON'T BE ABSURD! I'M NOT A MONSTER. OF COURSE I WOULD.

HOW TO GIVE AND RECEIVE A COMPLIMENT

When you give a compliment, you say something that's true and specific, and it makes the other person feel good. (Beware of the "backhanded compliment," which is when you somehow suggest that there was, or is still, a problem.)

YES

I LOVE YOUR NEW GLASSES!

THANK YOU!

NO

ALSO NO

Getting a compliment can be strangely challenging. Even if you're thrilled, you might feel really shy and awkward when someone says something nice to you, and this awkward feeling can lead you to respond in a way that might actually make the other person feel bad or silly for having complimented you.

Instead, try simply saying, "Thank you so much!" or "I love that you noticed!" or "You just made my day!" You can offer a compliment back if you're genuinely inspired to—but you absolutely don't need to.

POP QUIZ

You're going on a field trip to the
Museum of Weird Smells. *Yay!*
You've been assigned a seatmate
you don't know. *Yikes!* What do you do?

1 Clutch your chest, pretend to have a heart attack,
and stagger to the nurse's office.

2 Squinch your eyes shut and snore softly for the
whole ride.

3 Introduce yourself and have a conversation.

4 Introduce yourself and sit quietly.

Answer: 3 or 4. It's friendly to introduce yourself, but
you don't have to talk to someone just because they're
there! It's fine to be quiet if that's how you're feeling; the
other person might be feeling that way, too.

CHAPTER 3

HOW TO GET ALONG WITH PEOPLE

Getting along with people means responding thoughtfully as differences come up. Because we're just humans! We disagree sometimes. We're right. We're wrong. We need to meet in the middle. And along the way, we need to remember to say *Thank you*, *You're right*, and *I'm so lucky*.

HOW TO
COMPROMISE

When you compromise with someone, you **meet each other halfway**—like how sandwiches were invented as a meeting place between a baloney lover and a bread baker.* Visualize it as taking a step toward someone else's idea at the same time as they're taking a step toward yours.

*Not actually how sandwiches were invented

A compromise might look like **picking a middle option**.

HMMM. YOU WANT TO PAINT THE PIÑATA YELLOW AND I WANT TO PAINT IT RED. SHOULD WE PAINT IT . . . ORANGE?

Nerd Fact

Co- and *com-* are prefixes that mean "together with." Think of words like cooperate or coworker. In this case, *compromise* means to, um . . . "promise together"? That doesn't actually make a ton of sense, but you get the gist.

Or a compromise might look like **taking turns**.

	MOM	BEN	DAD	BIRDY	TOTAL
TOSS A FRISBEE AROUND	3	5	1	4	13
DRAW PICTURES OF GHOSTS 👻	5	4	3	5	(17)
WATCH CAT VIDEOS	2	2	5	3	12
MAKE DUMPLINGS	4	3	4	2	13
CLEAN THE GARAGE	1	1	2	1	5

WINNER!

← MAJOR LOSER

A fun compromise strategy is "ranked choice": When you're trying to decide about something, write down all the options. Then each person assigns a number to each one in descending order from their top choice to their bottom choice. Add up all the numbers, and the highest-scoring option wins.

HOW TO GIVE SOMEONE THE BENEFIT OF THE DOUBT

When you give someone the benefit of the doubt, you **assume they're doing their best** and you lean toward the most positive interpretation of their situation or behavior. Maybe a person seems unfriendly, but really they're just shy; maybe someone who suddenly acts weird is going through something hard you don't know about.

Let's say your friend texts to cancel a plan at the last minute. When you don't give them the benefit of the doubt, you might feel bad (we call this "hurting your own feelings") and you might make them feel bad, too.

WRONG

ASHER

I CAN'T WALK DIESEL WITH YOU TODAY

UGH I KNEW YOU SECRETLY HATED MY DOG

When you give someone the benefit of the doubt, you assume they have a good reason or that something's going on.

Assuming the best about people gives everyone a little more space to make mistakes and be imperfect. (But if someone keeps doing something that hurts or upsets you, then it might be time to change your expectations about what that person has to offer.)

RIGHT

HOW TO
BE WRONG

Were you wrong about something? Maybe an actual fact, or even something bigger, like the way you handled conflict? Just say it.

Or this way:

If you were wrong about something bigger, say so.

*See How to Apologize on page 70.

Nerd Fact

In her book *The Gift of Failure*, author Jessica Lahey writes a lot about the benefits, especially for young people, of making mistakes and learning from them. She describes miscalculations, setbacks, mistakes, and failures as "the very experiences that teach [kids] how to be resourceful, persistent, innovative, and resilient citizens of this world." Wow! That really *is* a gift.

HOW TO
BE RIGHT

Were you right about something? Share your knowledge or expertise, by all means, but try not to gloat (which means acting all pleased with yourself about your own rightness). And remember that being right is usually less important than being kind. (Sigh.)

WRONG
(unless it will make the other person laugh)

WHO KNEW HOW MUCH AN ELEPHANT POOP WEIGHED?

me!

I DID!

YOU DIDN'T!

HAH!

YOU SAID 10 POUNDS!

TRY 3 TIMES THAT AMOUNT!

RIGHT

OH, HEY, REMEMBER OUR CONVERSATION AT THE ZOO? I WAS ACTUALLY RIGHT ABOUT ELEPHANT POOP. IT REALLY DOES WEIGH OVER 30 POUNDS ON AVERAGE. I LOOKED IT UP.

But if someone *constantly* treats you like you don't know what you're talking about—and you *do* know what you're talking about—then feel free to stand up for yourself and communicate your knowledge as vigorously as you need to.

JUST SAYING. Learning how to be right and wrong is like learning to be a gracious winner and a gracious loser. In other words, you don't run around saying "Three cheers for me!" for a week or lie down on the field cryingly until they drag you off. Even if you kind of want to.

HOW TO
ARGUE

When you disagree with someone else and you talk about it, that's an argument—even if you're just expressing your difference of opinion and aren't angry. You might argue with a friend about the rules of Uno or with your sister about whether or not your dog can do math.

Some arguments need to be resolved before you can move forward (like the game rules), and others can just hang there without getting resolved.

If you get stuck, try one of these strategies:

Turn to outside sources like Wikipedia, the game rules, a book about the subject, or a person who knows a lot about the topic.

Think to yourself "Maybe I'm wrong" and try saying it out loud.

Give up the idea of winning and work more on listening to and connecting with the other person. Relationships are more important than being right.

Try to find common ground (something you can agree on) even if you can't agree on everything. (See How to Compromise on page 46.)

Agree to disagree. This is a friendly way of deciding you can't come to a consensus about this particular topic, and it can be a good way to end an argument that's no longer fun or useful.

This type of resolution won't always work: You might agree to disagree about low-stakes issues (mushrooms vs. pepperoni as the best pizza topping), but when injustice is at the heart of your disagreement (racism, say), then you shouldn't casually compromise in this way. (See Chapter 7 for more ways to think about this.)

I GUESS WE'LL REALLY NEVER KNOW WHO IS RIGHT . . . WE CAN'T SEE INSIDE HIS HEAD.

JUST SAYING. Posting on social media is, of course, another kind of "saying," and you want to think carefully about what you say there, too—not just because the internet is read both by robots and by actual, real-life, feelings-having people, but also because once something is online, it's very hard to get rid of.

HOW TO PERSUADE SOMEONE

Sometimes you really want to convince someone to do or think something: a teacher, about letting you report on a book that's not included in their list; a parent, about getting a pet lizard; or a friend, about an important belief you hold.

Start with that old favorite word—*PLEASE*—then try this:

Speak calmly and respectfully—stopping to listen to the other person—while you build your case.

PLEASE CAN WE GET A LIZARD?

I READ AN ARTICLE THAT KIDS WITH PETS DEVELOP HEALTHY, RESPONSIBLE HABITS.

KIDS WITH PETS STUDY HARDER!

DRAW ON DATA OR RESEARCH

DRAW ON PAST EXPERIENCE

REMEMBER WHEN WE GOT PETEY THE GOLDFISH? AND I TOOK SUCH GOOD CARE OF HIM?

DRAW ON YOUR OWN PASSION

I'VE BEEN TALKING ABOUT WANTING A LIZARD SINCE PRESCHOOL.

POP QUIZ

You lost at Monopoly. (Darn that hotel on Park Place!) Now your little brother is challenging you to play again, and you don't want to. What do you do?

1 Cry too hard to answer him. Also, he wouldn't be able to hear you over the sound of your fists pounding the ground.

2 Say, "No way," and accuse him of cheating.

3 Say, "That was fun, but I think I've had enough getting my butt kicked for now!"

4 Say, "I've probably had enough Monopoly. But I'd play something else!"

Answer: 3 or 4. You don't have to play Monopoly again (thank goodness), but you can still be a good loser and, if you like, compromise on a new activity.

HOW TO
BE GRATEFUL

Expressing gratitude is such an important skill—not just because it will make people feel good about being generous and helpful toward you, but also because it's scientifically proven to make you happier. Are there people in your life who do nice things for you? (There are.) Make a habit of noticing and acknowledging them!

NOT THIS

BUT THIS

JUST SAYING. Did your friend bring you a hot chocolate? That's so nice! You can just say "Thank you so much!" or send them a bursting-heart emoji. But if your grandma knit you a whole entire blanket that probably took her, like, 20 years? Go ahead and spend the 5 minutes it will take to write her an actual **thank-you note**. She will be so, so happy—and she deserves to be.

CHAPTER 4

HOW TO DEAL WITH HARD THINGS

These are the stickier situations: You're needing to express difficult feelings or deal with other people's difficult feelings—or both. It's okay. Try to be the best version of yourself you can be, and at the end of the day, you'll feel like you did what you could to make it right.

HOW TO
BE EMBARRASSED

Did you do the most awkward thing—like, you wish a UFO would swoop down and scoop you up so you don't have to be on the planet for one more terrible second? Yeah. We do that stuff, too. Like, all the time. Luckily, responding to it is easy!

There are two simple, all-purpose choices for any awkward situation:

EXCUSE ME!

I'M SO SORRY.

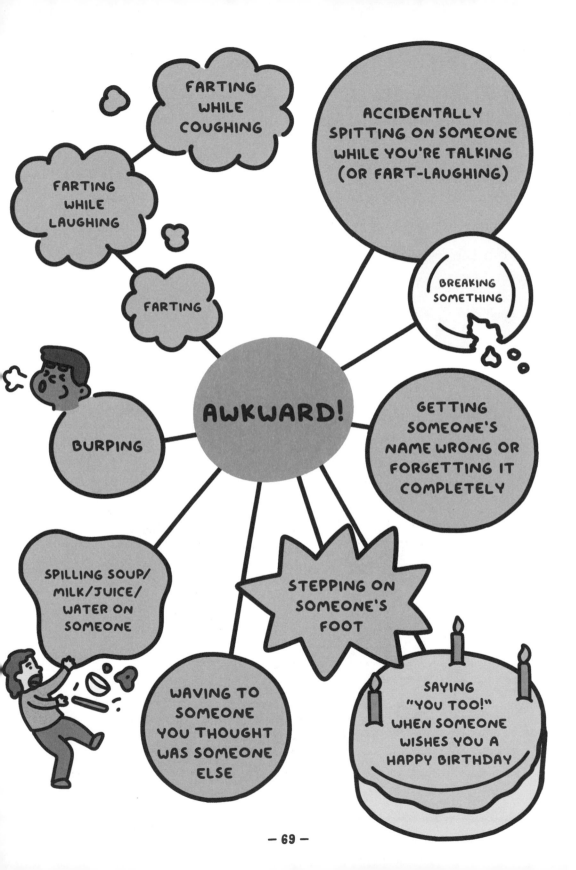

HOW TO
APOLOGIZE

We make mistakes all the time! It's not a big deal—unless we hurt someone in the process. Even then, though, the most important thing is not what you did; it's what you do next. Say, "I'm sorry," and empathize with the person you hurt, which means trying to **imagine what it feels like to be them**. Then see what you can do to make it better.

WRONG

WHATEVER. IF IT'S A CRIME TO EAT A BANANA, THEN I'M GUILTY AS CHARGED!

DO NOT EAT

Some apologies are a bigger deal than others. You might text an "lol sorry" to your mom because you forgot to take out the trash. But if you hurt your best friend's feelings? That's going to require a more thoughtful and heartfelt interaction: "I'm so sorry. I can see that I really hurt your feelings, and I wish I hadn't."

RIGHT

I'M REALLY SORRY.
IT MUST BE SO FRUSTRATING
THAT I ATE THE BANANA FROM
YOUR SCIENCE EXPERIMENT
ON RIPENING. I WASN'T PAYING
ATTENTION. CAN I BIKE
TO THE STORE AND
GET YOU A NEW ONE?

HOW TO
FORGIVE

Picture letting go of your bad feelings, like a bunch of balloons that floats away into the sky (but somehow doesn't end up littering or harming any animals). Aaahhh! That's forgiveness.

Remember empathizing, from two pages ago? So, yeah. Empathy is at the root of forgiveness, too: "I see you. Who you are, not just what you did. I don't want you to feel bad." It's generous to forgive, and it will make you feel better, too—even if you still ask the other person to right a wrong or hold them accountable for their actions.

RIGHT

I'M SO SORRY MY GUM FLEW INTO YOUR HAIR! I DIDN'T REALIZE I WAS LAUGHING THAT HARD.

THAT'S OKAY. I'VE DONE THAT, TOO. I NEEDED TO TRIM MY BANGS ANYWAY!

ALSO RIGHT

I'M SORRY I TOOK MONEY FROM YOUR PIGGY BANK.

I FORGIVE YOU. PLEASE JUST PAY IT BACK, AND IF YOU EVER NEED TO BORROW ANY, ASK ME NEXT TIME.

Nerd Fact

"To err is human; to forgive, divine" is an old quote (Alexander Pope, 1711) that basically means "Everyone makes mistakes, but forgiving someone is really special."

HOW TO
BE ANGRY

Being your best kind and compassionate self doesn't mean you don't get to be angry. You do.

   If you're mad *about something*—but not *at someone*—then make sure you don't take it out on a nearby person. Do confide in a friend or family member, though.

Or try one of these feelings-releasers:

Tear paper into tiny shreds

Go for a walk or run

Punch a pillow

Jump on a trampoline

Meditate

Cuddle with your pets

Breathe deeply

Pop bubble wrap

Scream, laugh, or cry

And if you're mad *at someone*? Tell them why, without shouting, name-calling, or using words like "always" or "never." Try starting your sentence with the word "I" to remind them (and yourself) that this is a feeling you're having, not a deep fact about them that's bad.

WRONG

RIGHT

YOU ALWAYS STEAL MY WAFFLES OUT OF THE TOASTER! BECAUSE YOU'RE A WAFFLE-STEALING PAIN IN MY WAFFLE HOLE!

I'M MAD THAT YOU ATE THE WAFFLE I TOASTED.

Nerd Fact

Anger can release adrenaline, the fight-flight-or-freeze hormone. Adrenaline can speed up your heart, make you shake, or make you breathe in a weird way. It's okay! Breathe deeply or do something physical. Your body will get rid of the adrenaline, and you will feel (and look) like yourself again.

Sometimes you will need to **stick up for yourself**. Maybe a teacher didn't add up your quiz score correctly, the dad you babysit for underpaid you, a stranger is standing too close to you on the bus, or a parent has accused you of doing something you didn't do.

First, give the person the benefit of the doubt (page 50) by assuming they made a mistake or didn't understand the impact of what they were doing. (If there's a bigger injustice at issue—say, a racist assumption—you might not be in a benefit-of-the-doubt kind of space. See How to Disrupt Prejudice on page 134.)

Next, explain—politely and clearly—what needs to happen to correct it.

If you need backup, ask a friend or family member for support.

GIVING THE BENEFIT OF THE DOUBT

EXPLAINING WHAT NEEDS TO HAPPEN NEXT

HOW TO SAY NO

Another way you may need to advocate for yourself is by saying no to things you can't or don't want to do. This is an important skill to learn. Because even if you want to be a person who says yes to lots of things—like helping and volunteering and joining in and keeping someone company—you also need to take care of yourself.

You might have a good, obvious reason to not do something, or you might just not want to. Both are valid.

You'll want to be clear when you say no, and, assuming someone is not pressuring or bullying you, you'll also want to be kind. This can be a hard combo to nail.

NAILING IT

THANK YOU SO MUCH FOR INVITING ME TO YOUR FAMILY'S SARDINE PARTY. I CAN'T COME TONIGHT, BUT MAYBE ANOTHER TIME.

ALSO NAILING IT

I'M ACTUALLY ALLERGIC TO FISH,* SO I'M GOING TO SKIP. BUT THANK YOU FOR INCLUDING ME!

*Say this only if you're allergic to fish.

HOW TO
ASK FOR HELP

Independence is overrated! We all need help—lots of it, and frequently. So go ahead and ask your math teacher to work through a hard problem with you, ask your sister for a hug after a hard day, ask your aunt to show you a guitar chord, or simply ask for another set of hands when a job is too big for you to do alone. To show the person (or people) that you respect their time and appreciate their assistance, be sure to express your gratitude by thanking them.

Nerd Fact

Help is such an important part of human life that there are, like, a million sayings about it:

- "Many hands make light work."

- "It takes a village."

- "Teamwork makes the dream work."

- And, as my daughter likes to say, "A bird in the hand is easier to get if you have another hand helping you get the bird into it." (**Note:** This is not an actual saying.)

HOW TO
SHUT DOWN GOSSIP

Saying nasty stuff behind people's backs is not only unkind and untrustworthy—it also feels bad. Plus, you don't want to worry that your friends are going to gossip about you next. So don't do it! Walking away is fine; shutting it down is better. Be courageous, be funny (if you want), and turn the conversation in a positive direction instead.

. . . AND THEN SHE STARTED DANCING, AND I WAS LIKE, "OH MY GOD, SHE IS SO TRAGIC."

BUT DON'T YOU LOVE THAT SHE WAS SO BRAVE? I MEAN, I'M BOUNCING UP AND DOWN LIKE A BROKEN POGO STICK, AND SHE'S JUST OUT THERE WITH IT, FEELING THE MUSIC. I THINK SHE'S KIND OF FABULOUS, HONESTLY.

POSITIVE "GOSSIP"

Okay, this isn't actually a thing, but it's what we like to call the habit of talking behind people's backs about how awesome they are. It's basically the opposite of behind-someone's-back nastiness, and it feels great and nourishes trust in your community.

HOW TO
LET A FRIEND GO

Some friendships are lifelong (that's that second *F* in BFF), and some aren't. That's okay, but it can be painful when a friendship ends.

If you're sad that a friend seems to be drifting from you—they're not returning your texts or saving you a seat or making plans with you—first see if there's a misunderstanding you can clear up.

DID I DO OR SAY ANYTHING TO UPSET YOU?

If there's not, then take a deep breath—and let them go. It doesn't have to be dramatic, and it's okay to still be glad to see them (if you are). But **you're also allowed to feel sad**, and to seek comfort from your friends, family, and pets. Relationships sometimes change, but you are still lovable and loved.

GHOSTING

Ghosting refers to the practice of ending a relationship by disappearing suddenly from a person's life, with no explanation or communication. Ghosting someone is unkind and irresponsible (unless that person has harmed you or refused to acknowledge information you've tried to share clearly). The other person is stuck feeling confused and wondering what happened, instead of understanding and moving on. So please don't do this to anyone.

And if someone does it to you? Reach out to establish that there's not a misunderstanding or miscommunication— and then let them go. You are a worthy person who deserves better.

HOW TO
STEP BACK FROM A FRIENDSHIP

If you've stopped enjoying someone's company, you are not obligated to remain friends with that person—but you *are* obligated to be compassionate and respectful.

Don't gossip about them; don't be unkind; and don't be sometimes friendly and sometimes not, which is confusing. You can stop reaching out and hope they feel the same way, or you can talk through it if they ask for an explanation.

POP QUIZ

Your brother found you drying the dog with his special favorite towel—the one that has his name spelled out in candy corns—and now he's mad. What do you say?

1 "Sorry I took Rufus for a walk in the rain! You're welcome, actually."

2 "Wait. This is *your* towel?"

3 "Did you want Rufus to step all over your stuff with wet paws?"

4 "I'm sorry! I just grabbed a towel without thinking. Let me pop it in the laundry."

Answer: 4. Take responsibility, apologize, and see what you can do to make it right.

CHAPTER 5

HOW TO BE IN A ROMANTIC RELATIONSHIP (OR NOT)

- -

Maybe you've got a crush or you're actually dating* someone—or maybe you're not interested in a more-than-friends relationship now (or ever). Every one of those things is just perfect! And so are all of the different ways you might experience or express your gender or sexuality. Feel free, of course, to skip this chapter if you know it's not your thing right now.

* We do use the term "dating" to keep things simple, even though it's a word that might make you cringe. We're sorry.

HOW TO KNOW IF YOU HAVE A CRUSH ON SOMEONE

You might feel similar about a friend and a crush: trusting, connected, and happy when they're around. So how can you tell the difference?

A crush might give you a kind of fizzy feeling. If a friend is a tall glass of delicious, thirst-quenching water, then a crush might be more like a drink with bubbles in it.

Do you feel excited in your stomach when you see them? That might be a crush. Do you go out of your way to run into them? That might be a crush, too.

OH! HI!

You don't have to do anything about a crush. You can just keep it to yourself, like a fun secret that's kind of distracting.

Or you can find out if they feel the same way about you! (This is much easier than trying to interpret their one-word text for 3 hours.)

If they don't, you can simply evaporate into thin air! Oh, wait. No, you can't. But even if you're kind of dying of awkwardness, that feeling will pass more quickly than you might imagine.

Nerd Fact

Your brain makes two specific hormones, dopamine and oxytocin, when you have a crush on someone. Dopamine makes you feel good, which is one reason why you might seek that person out all the time. And oxytocin, also called "the love hormone," gives you that warm, cozy feeling that you might also get from your pets. Who knew that neuroscience was so romantic? (Okay, a crush can also fill you with the hormone adrenaline, which makes you feel more panicky than lovey-dovey, but still.)

HOW TO
ASK SOMEONE OUT

You have a crush! And you think that just maybe(!) they've got one back. What next? Well, you can see if they might want to hang out sometime, which you can ask in person, in a handwritten note, over text, or however else feels right. (Skywriting! Invisible ink!)

If your crush is already a friend, how you ask might be different.

ASKING OUT A FRIEND

ASKING OUT AN ACQUAINTANCE

JUST SAYING. If someone asks you out on a date and you don't want to go? You never, ever have to. Your job is to be your most authentic self—not to please other people. You can say, "I'm not interested in dating right now," or "I really value our friendship," or simply "No, but thank you for asking." Whatever feels clear, respectful, and most comfortable to you is fine.

HOW TO
GO ON A DATE

It doesn't matter what you've heard or read about dating; whatever you like to do, *that's* what you should do on a date.

It could be spending time on a shared interest, like music or skateboarding or video games or sweet potato fries.

Or you could take turns introducing each other to your favorite things: playing Jenga, walking your Chihuahua, making collages, or baking meringues.

If you're not sure what to do or what to expect, just say that. Good, honest communication is more important than anything else.

JUST SAYING. Doing a specific fun activity together is much easier and less pressured-feeling than just "hanging out."

WHAT IF YOU'RE LGBTQ+?

Whatever your gender or sexuality, dating is the same! Unless you're experiencing discrimination or bullying, in which case the part that's you and your person is still the same (yay!), but there's a sucky extra layer of dealing with other people's horribleness (yuck). Seek out the support of an adult you trust—a guidance counselor, parent, teacher, or friend—to strategize about safety so you can save more of your energy for the fun part of dating.

HOW TO
DEAL WITH BEING AWKWARD

What? You're awkward on a date? That's weird. Just kidding! *Of course* you're awkward! It's not some filtered Instagram slideshow where you go ice-skating and there are rose petals everywhere and it's snowing and everybody's skin looks mysteriously great. It's real, actual life.

Fill awkward silences with questions, either deep ones ("Do you think there's an afterlife?") or goofy ones ("If it couldn't be sand, would you rather a beach be made of glass pebbles or jelly beans?"). The curiosity sparks on page 34 can be useful here.

Invite the messy, not-perfect, authentic YOU to your date. You don't need to pretend, and you don't need to play it cool. Be honest about any awkwardness.

HOW TO
BREAK UP WITH SOMEONE

Breaking up with someone might feel a little like stepping back from a friendship (see page 86), but it requires more clarity. It also requires being true to yourself and what you want while still supporting the other person's self-esteem.

If you want to stay (or become) friends, say so. It's only because of movies or weird cultural ideas that we are led to believe that friendship is somehow a lesser option than a romantic relationship. It's not—and you can say as much.

I DON'T THINK THIS RELATIONSHIP IS WORKING FOR ME AS A ROMANCE, BUT I REALLY WANT TO BE FRIENDS WITH YOU. AND MY FRIENDS ARE ACTUALLY THE MOST IMPORTANT PEOPLE TO ME IN THE WORLD.

But if you've figured out that you actually don't enjoy the person's company? Then friendship isn't going to be so great either, to be honest, so don't offer it.

HOW TO
GET YOUR
HEART BROKEN

Dating, like friendship, involves making yourself vulnerable in a particular way. Which means you can get hurt. Lots of our advice about letting go of a friendship (page 84) applies here, too, like seeking comfort from friends, family, and pets—and understanding that you're still loved and lovable.

Remember, even though it's the most annoying thing to hear, that **the best cure for heartbreak is *time***. You will simply feel better as the bad feelings fade and happier feelings take their place.

Notice (maybe for the first time) that a lot of your favorite songs and books and movies involve people's hearts getting broken. Do you know why? Because *it's not just you.* It happens to most people. And even though it's hard to accept rejection, that's what you have to do.

Also, while you're dating, remember to **hold on to your own self**—your self-love, your self-worth, your own friends and interests—because you're always going to be there, before, during, and after any relationship you're in.

HOW TO
NOT BE IN A ROMANTIC RELATIONSHIP

Despite the impression you might be getting from books, the internet, and romantic comedies, lots of people your age *aren't* dating (and that's true whatever age you are). If you're not in a relationship with someone—or don't even want to be—you're not weird, and you're not alone.

You don't need a reason for not wanting to date, but there are lots:

- Your friends and family are meeting all of your emotional needs.

- You don't feel ready to be in an intimate or romantic relationship.

- Dating isn't going to be your thing until much later—or ever, if you identify as asexual or aromantic (meaning *not* sexual or *not* romantic).

- Dating conflicts with your faith or values.

- You haven't met the right person, or you *have* met them and you still don't want to date them. (Or they don't want to date you.)

- You're just busy with friends, school, hockey, complicated guitar chords, political activism, or learning to make fancy French pastries. You know, *life*.

Someone you like asks if you want to hang out (like *hang out* hang out). What do you say?

1 I'd love to.

2 I'd love to—but, just so you know, I'm not really into dating anyone right now.

3 Oh, I can't! We're celebrating my guinea pig's birthday that night. But you'd be welcome to come!

4 I don't, but thank you so much for asking me.

IT'S MY BIRTHDAY!

Answer: 1, 2, 3, or 4. There are no wrong answers here, as long as you're true to what you want and respectful of the person asking.

CHAPTER 6

HOW TO BE SUPPORTIVE

- -

We all need to feel loved! That's just what people are like. You can make such a huge difference to the people in your life—your friends and family and classmates and even people you don't know especially well—by being there when things are good . . . and when things aren't so good, too.

HOW TO SHOW YOUR APPRECIATION

One way to support the people you care about is to fill up their storage of positivity—then, if they're ever feeling down, they can remember something you said or did that made them feel good about themselves.

There are lots of ways to do this—mostly by being a steady, loving presence in their lives—but here are some specific ones:

Pay a compliment.

Express random gratitude for the fact of this person existing.

To:	Linh Tran
Subject:	How Are You?

Hi, Aunt Linh,

I woke up thinking about how I was the luckiest nephew ever to have you for my aunt. Just feeling grateful for everything you do for me.

Text a photo and/or a loving message.

HOW TO
EXPRESS EMPATHY

Empathy means trying to understand what someone else is feeling. (It's different from *sympathy*, which means that you feel sorry for them without imagining their experience.) If someone feels bad, empathy is a gift you can share.

"I can imagine how sad that must feel" or "I can imagine how hard that is," you can say. (Instead of "Poor you.")

"I like spending time with you even when you're sad," you can say. (Instead of "Cheer up.")

"Tell me more—I'm listening," you can say. (Instead of "You'll feel better" or "That doesn't sound like a big deal.")

"I can see you're really hurting," you can say. (Instead of "It's okay.")

It can be helpful to remind the person that they'll feel better with time—or it can be annoying. When in doubt, offer a hug, a tissue, or just your patient presence. Know that they might be feeling really comforted, even if you can't see it.

You might also express empathy by how you choose to *act* in a situation that's difficult for someone:

The new kid alone at lunch: You sit with them because you know how that feels (or at least you can imagine it).

A person on the bus who has a visible mobility issue or who's holding lots of bags or a wiggly baby: You offer your seat because you can imagine how hard it would be to stand if your body wasn't feeling strong or if your hands were full.

An organization collecting toys for kids living unhoused at the holidays: You donate a toy because you can imagine how sad it would feel not to get anything.

Anyone who's sad or struggling: You offer a hug, a tissue, a listening ear, or some quiet company because you know how comforting that can feel when you're sad or struggling.

HOW TO
BE SUPPORTIVE WHEN SOMEONE CONFIDES IN YOU

If someone shares something important with you, then you should skip around feeling great about yourself because you are such a good and trustworthy friend! You really are. Oh, but also, you'll want to respond to them in a thoughtful way. You can thank them for trusting you enough to tell you, be happy if they're happy, or offer support or advice if they need it.

When someone tells you something, remember that they might not have shared this information with everyone. First listen without interrupting. And then ask any clarifying questions you need to.

JUST SAYING. If you're gay and coming out, hooray! And remember that if the person you come out to has any biases, those are theirs to deal with—not yours. This is about *you*, and you are perfect just the way you are.

HOW TO
COMFORT SOMEONE

Compassion is basically empathy put into action. When you try to make someone feel better while reassuring them that they can still have all their feelings? That's compassion—and it's basically what it means to comfort someone.

People need to be comforted for all kinds of reasons, big and small: They didn't win their soccer game or get a part in the play; a person or pet they cared about died; someone was unkind to them; injustice in the world feels overwhelming; their parents are splitting up; they're not feeling physically or emotionally well; or a reason they don't choose to share.

You might already know how to best comfort a friend or family member, or you might have to ask.

SETTING BOUNDARIES

Your goal is to be supportive, of course. But sometimes a person—either someone you don't know all that well or someone you're close to—can ask too much of you or expect you to keep secrets that are too hard (or not safe) to keep. If you find yourself overwhelmed by someone else's need for support or think that they are being hurt (or are hurting someone else), ask for help from a trusted adult or a school counselor.

Here are some things you can do, depending on the person and situation:

Offer to listen.

Check if they need a snack.

Bring them a blanket, a pet, a teddy bear, or a cup of tea.

Send them a text that says, "I'm thinking of you."

Make them laugh.

See if they'd like a hug.

Remind them that it's totally okay to cry or be sad.

HOW TO
BE INCLUSIVE

If you notice someone being left out of things, you have the power to include them—which is a wonderful way to exercise your empathy muscle, because you probably know what it feels like to be excluded (rotten) and what a relief it is to be looped in by someone's kindness (phew).

Ask a kid sitting alone if they'd like to join your lunch table (they might not take you up on it, of course, since plenty of folks are happy to sit alone); remember to never exclude one person from a large group; and make valentines for the whole class, even if you haven't had to do that since kindergarten. It's honestly so much easier and more rewarding to be inclusive and feel good about yourself than to do the opposite.

OH, THANKS! I'D LOVE TO.

HOW TO STICK UP FOR SOMEONE

You know when something isn't right, like when someone is being teased, picked on, laughed at, accused of something you know they didn't do, or treated unfairly. And it takes *so much courage*, but you can help.

Start by making sure they want your help. "Can I help?" is something you can always ask. Or even "How can I help?" If they don't want your help, stand back, but say, "I'm here if you need me."

Describe the problem to the people who are making it
("That's mean," say, or "That's not fair"), then explain what you want to happen next ("Leave him alone," say, or "Listen to his side of the story," or simply "Stop").

Or ignore them and encourage the person you're sticking up for to walk away with you. You can create a distraction, if you need to, by dropping your books, having a coughing fit, or saying a made-up reason ("Come on, we gotta go to that meeting, remember?"). This might help the situation feel less intense to everyone so that you can get out of it more easily.

Don't worry what other people think. You are doing the right thing.

Be extra kind to the person who's been picked on to remind them that they're not alone.

If it feels too big to handle, or not safe, then get a teacher, a parent, or another trusted adult to step in and help.

BULLYING

If someone is trying to hurt or scare you or somebody else, either in person or online, you should tell a trusted adult—even if the bully threatens you or tells you not to. If the first adult you tell doesn't help you, then tell a different one. The website **StopBullying.gov** has resources for what to do if you're being bullied or if someone else is and how to help create a safer environment at your school and online.

HOW TO
GIVE ADVICE

Someone in your life isn't sure what they should do next! And, lucky for them, you're here to help. But how?

The first thing you could do is find out if they actually *want* advice—which you can do by asking.

> DO YOU WANT MY HELP FIGURING THIS OUT? OR DO YOU JUST WANT TO TALK THROUGH IT AND I'LL LISTEN? EITHER IS FINE!

If they do want advice, then you can ask if it would be helpful to make a pros and cons list about the decision or issue they're facing.

Express your confidence in the person's ability to make a good decision. **This might actually be the very best way to help.**

I KNOW THIS IS A HARD DECISION, BUT YOU'LL MAKE A GOOD ONE! AND YOU CAN ALWAYS MAKE A DIFFERENT DECISION LATER IF YOU NEED TO.

Your friend wanted to be cast as Juliet, and instead she's "A Potted Plant on the Balcony." She is crying when she tells you. What do you do?

1 Say, "What?" because you're watching a video of dancing broccoli.

2 Say, "That's a dumb thing to be sad about."

3 Give her a tissue and say, "I'm sorry. That's so disappointing. You're such a good actor, and I know you really wanted that part."

4 Say, "But who's going to crush it and be the best plant ever in the history of Shakespeare's plants?"

Answer: 3. Honor her sadness and offer comfort. (If you know it will make her laugh, and that she will want to laugh, you can add 4, too.)

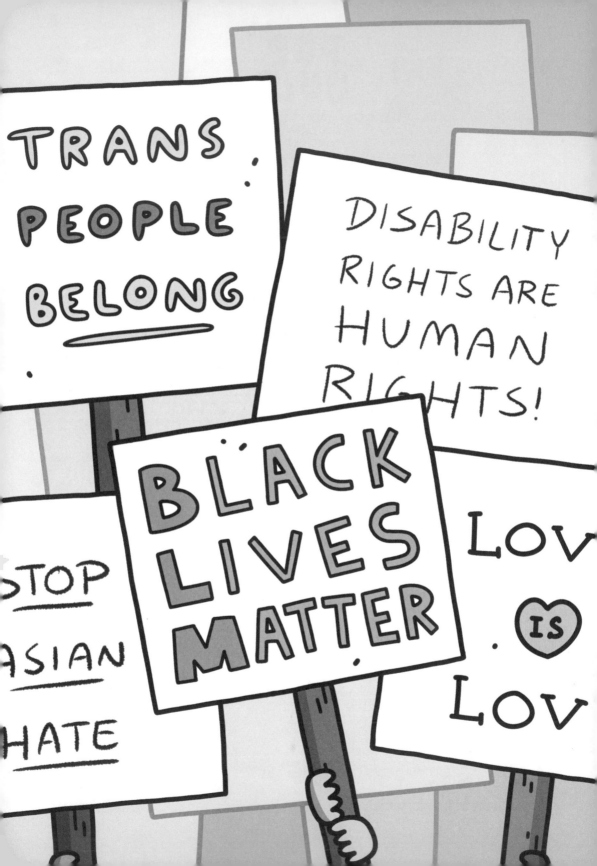

CHAPTER 7

HOW TO BE AN ALLY

- - - - - - - - - - - - - - - - - - - -

An ally is someone who commits to supporting people who are being discriminated against. You might be an ally to people with disabilities if you don't have a disability, an ally to people of color if you're white, or an ally to other people who are fighting mistreatment using whatever privilege and power you have. As you probably already know, allyship is hard, important work.

HOW TO
BE COURAGEOUS

The kinds of interactions this chapter is asking you to have might make you feel nervous or uncomfortable. And while that feeling might typically be a sign that something about what you're doing is wrong, in this case, it's usually a sign that you're doing good work. Here are some ideas that might help you feel braver.

Remember that **you can't control how other people act**. What you can control is how—and when and whether—you act. As an ally, you will know, at the end of the day, that you did the right thing. It's okay to feel awkward or anxious in the process—this is hard, uncomfortable work—but make sure you feel safe and supported in the interaction, or ask an adult for help.

SPEAKING UP EVEN THOUGH SHE HAS BUTTERFLIES IN HER STOMACH

As with learning a language, an instrument, a sport, or really any other thing that's worth doing, **practice helps**. The more you stand up and speak out, the better at it you'll be.

You're not trying to be right. You're trying to share, learn, and make the world safer for everyone.

If you're not sure what to do, **try asking a question**. "What did you mean when you said that?"

It's okay to make mistakes. That's where some of the learning happens. You'll screw up, you'll apologize—and then you'll keep trying, the same way that if you tripped halfway up a mountain you wouldn't just turn around and head back down. You'd stand back up and keep going.

Nerd Fact

In *Why We Act*, a book she wrote about why people do and don't act in situations that call for action, the psychologist Catherine Sanderson uses the term "moral rebel" to describe people who are willing to call out bad behavior, even if it means doing something different from people around them who aren't doing anything. Being a moral rebel feels like a good goal, right?

HOW TO
EDUCATE YOURSELF

Being a good ally means working to understand the identities and experiences of the folks you're supporting. This can mean a lot of different things, such as:

Being a good listener when someone shares their experience of prejudice or discrimination with you. Really listening means paying attention to the other person and imagining their experience, rather than thinking only about how what they're telling you makes you feel.

Trying not to get defensive about your own privilege or power that comes to you simply because you fit a specific social group. You'll learn more if you listen with an open mind rather than jumping in to say, "Not all white people/men/straight people do that."

Asking questions to further your understanding of that experience

instead of making assumptions about it. Of course, if the person doesn't feel like educating you or saying more, that's okay, too. (They might be tired of explaining everything.)

Reading books and articles about issues such as racism, sexism, or religious persecution, written by people who have firsthand experience with these kinds of discrimination.

Reading books and articles that celebrate the history of, say, Black people, Indigenous people, Islam, or the disability rights movement.

Looking up terms or issues you don't know or don't understand.

READ ON

To read more about effective allyship, check out *Stamped: Racism, Antiracism, and You*, by Jason Reynolds and Ibram X. Kendi, and *This Book Is Anti-Racist: 20 Lessons on How to Wake Up, Take Action, and Do the Work*, by Tiffany Jewell.

INSTEAD OF MAKING AN ASSUMPTION

Nerd Fact

The word *ally* shares a root with the word *alliance*. They both come from the Latin *alligare*, which means "to bind together."

ASK A QUESTION

HOW TO
DISRUPT PREJUDICE

Change happens because people take action at all levels of society: not just in courts, government, and protests, but also in our own relationships and conversations. Here are some of the ways you might help eliminate discrimination:

Appreciate and respect difference. This means, among other things, remembering that racial, cultural, religious, and other differences are never themselves a problem—racism and bigotry are.

Attend (or organize) a protest, rally, sit-in, or vigil.
(See page 150 for more on how to be an activist.)

Write a letter or an email. This is especially useful for prejudice that happens at the institutional level, which means inside an organization. Even better, if you know someone from the impacted group, ask them if they're comfortable talking to you about what kinds of suggestions or requests might be helpful!

Dear Principal Milton,

I see you put up a Christmas tree in the middle school lobby. The Jewish students I talked to were upset about it. I'm writing to ask that the school adopt a more inclusive approach to the holiday season. Please let me know how you plan to address this issue.

Yours truly,
Jack

JUST SAYING. If a situation feels too threatening to you, it's okay not to speak up. Yes, it's really important to make the world a better place—but we need you safe and sound so you can keep doing that work.

Interrupt a conversation. If someone uses an offensive term or stereotype while they're talking, you can educate them about its history and impact. It might be most effective to start with a question: "Let me make sure I understand. What did you mean when you said that?"

Some research suggests that empathy—connecting with someone, sharing stories, and understanding where they're coming from—is a more successful way to change another person's mind than judgment.

SOMETIMES IT'S SUBTLE

Sometimes people do or say things that communicate a bias or stereotype in a confusing, indirect way, often without consciously intending to hurt someone. (You might also hear this referred to as a *racist microaggression*.) It's often a question or statement that appears to be friendly or curious but actually contains an oppressive assumption:

- "Your hair is actually really pretty!" (Suggests that this is a surprise.)

- "You speak English really well!" (Suggests that people of color usually *don't* speak English well.)

- "Where are you from?" (Suggests that people of color must be from somewhere else.)

If you've never experienced this, imagine these little jabs coming at you all the time, and how they could add up to a feeling that you were *less than*.

Then try to be certain that any question you ask or comment you make to a person of color is a question or comment you would make the same way to a white person.

HOW TO
RESPOND TO AN OFFENSIVE JOKE

One thing that's never funny is discrimination. And offensive jokes—whether they're racist or sexist or they engage other prejudices, such as ones about religion, bodies, or sexuality—are basically designed to make you laugh at a group of people who are or have been the targets of discrimination.

Whether a person makes a joke like that privately or it's in a TV show or on the internet, it does actual harm to people, either directly, by humiliating or scaring them, or indirectly, by continuing to put stereotypes and prejudice into the world.

A joke is tricky because the idea is that it's not meant to be serious (like one about a stinky dog), but discrimination *is* serious. If you laugh at the joke, then you're helping discrimination exist and spread, even if you know it's wrong. This can be really hard to deal with. Try giving the joke teller the benefit of the doubt by assuming they didn't mean to say something hurtful. Then be your bravest self, if you can, and ask a question or say what you noticed.

HOW TO
TALK ABOUT PRONOUNS

In a world where people are—yay!—feeling less limited to the sex they were assigned at birth or by labels such as "girl" and "boy" or "male" and "female," it is becoming increasingly common to say what pronouns* you use when you introduce yourself.

Saying what pronouns you use lets people know what gender you identify with (if any) and how to refer to you in conversation. Someone might cue you to this practice—"Hi! We're going to go around the circle. Please say your name and pronouns."—or you might think about introducing it yourself to help everyone feel more comfortable.

*Pronouns are those stand-in words like "he," "she," and "they" that people say when they're not repeating a person's name.

*These are gender-neutral pronouns, and they might mean that the person isn't either a boy or a girl and/or that they identify as a different gender. These folks might be nonbinary, agender, or gender fluid, or they might identify with a different term.

JUST SAYING. To address a group of people in a way that doesn't make any assumptions about gender, try saying *peeps*, *humans*, *friends*, or *folks*.

HOW TO
BE TRUSTWORTHY

Being a trustworthy ally will take practice. Here are some steps you can take:

- Listen without interrupting.

- Ask questions, but don't assume that the person you are talking to wants to spend their whole day teaching you about injustice—if there's more you want to learn about, make a mental note so you  can find a resource about it (librarians are super helpful).

- Use your privilege to fight injustice. (*Privilege*, in the context of social justice, means advantages you have that other people don't have.)

- Speak up and speak out—but don't speak *for* or *over* a group you don't belong to.

- Take responsibility for the mistakes you make.

- Don't call into question someone's experience of mistreatment. Understand that they might be angry or express other strong feelings that make you nervous or uncomfortable. Your job is to respect that person's feelings.

- Learn respectful language to use when referring to gender, sexuality, race, ethnicity, and physical and cognitive abilities.

POP QUIZ

Over lunch, a Muslim friend tells you that some other kids were making fun of her head scarf. What do you do?

1 Pretend to drop some food on the floor, then hide under the table until lunch is over.

2 Explain that she's overreacting—those kids were probably just kidding around!

3 Say, "Oh my god, the same thing happened to me! But, like, about my volleyball shorts."

4 Listen, and then affirm her experience: "I'm so sorry you had to go through that. Is there anything I can do to be helpful?"

Answer: 4. Being trustworthy means listening and validating a person's experience of prejudice—not turning away from it, not questioning their interpretation of it, and not making it be all about you. These are all hard things that take practice! That's okay. You have time.

I'M SO GLAD YOU JOINED US IN OUR PARK CLEANUP!
I LOVE THIS PARK AND I WANT OTHERS TO LOVE IT, TOO. I'M HAPPY TO VOLUNTEER.

CHAPTER 8

HOW TO CARE FOR YOUR COMMUNITY

Picture the concentric circles of your world: There's you in the middle, then your friends and family, your community, your town, state, country . . . the planet. You are part of all of these places, which means that you can have an impact on them all, too. Most of this book is about your immediate community, but in this chapter we're looking a little farther out.

HOW TO
BE A GOOD NEIGHBOR

Whether you're close with your neighbors or you just offer a wave from your side of the driveway or elevator, it's nice to be friendly. Plus, if they're older or alone or seem like they could use a hand, it's nice to be helpful, too. You could:

- Wheel their garbage can back after trash pickup.

- Offer to help with shoveling, mowing, or raking.

- Drop off cookies if you make extra. (Okay, yes, "extra" cookies aren't even a thing, but you know what we mean.)

THANKS!

- See if they need any errands run when you're biking into town.

DO YOU NEED ANYTHING?

IT'S OKAY, SPOTTY! I KNOW YOU'RE JUST EXCITED!

- Try not to be too aggravated by normal neighbor occurrences like an occasional barking dog or noisy bassoon practice.

BARK! BARK!

HOW TO
VOLUNTEER

When you volunteer to do something, you are basically saying to another person or your school or community: "What can I do to help?" or "I will!" or "I'd be happy to." Then you do something that benefits more people than just yourself. (Note: Volunteering is different from being volun-*told* to do something, which is when someone else volunteers you—like your mom saying, "I told Aunt Agnes you'd be happy to babysit the twins.")

NOT EXACTLY VOLUNTEERING

WHY, CERTAINLY!
I'D BE HAPPY TO EAT
THAT CHOCOLATE-COVERED
PRETZEL!

VOLUNTEERING

IF YOU STILL NEED
MORE PEOPLE FOR
THE BAKE SALE,
I'D BE HAPPY TO HELP.

Nerd Fact

Research suggests that volunteering releases dopamine, one of the neurochemicals that makes you feel happy. In other words, your brain will reward you for doing something good for other people! Good thinking, brain.

There are lots of ways to volunteer. You might:

Offer to help the person in your household who's **making dinner**.

I CAN HELP!

Join a volunteer program at your local hospital, animal shelter, religious organization, food pantry, soup kitchen, or senior center.

Donate food to a food drive or toys to a toy drive.

Pitch in when someone organizes a **cleanup of your neighborhood**, park, or local beach.

Contribute baked goods or car-washing to a **school fundraiser**.

Help your sister with her **math homework**.

HOW TO
BE AN ACTIVIST

Being an activist means fighting for political or social change to make the world safer and fairer for everybody. Activism approaches many of the same issues as volunteer work, but at a different level.

Volunteers often work to solve problems right here and now: People at the homeless shelter need warm clothes, so you run a coat drive. Activists often work to solve the problem at its root: The fact that there are so many people in the homeless shelter means your town needs more affordable housing, so you write a letter to your local government or newspaper.

HOUSING

To be an activist:

Figure out what problems you care most about and why. You might feel the same as or different from your family and friends about certain issues.

Find out who else is doing work around those issues and see what kinds of opportunities there are to get involved. Are people writing postcards to voters? Marching around their state capitol with protest signs? Calling their elected officials?

Decide where you're comfortable putting your energy. It's good to stretch past your point of total comfort—social justice work is often challenging—but you don't need to do anything that makes you feel panicky. You might want to chant a slogan, or you might feel more comfortable writing an email. Both are valid forms of activism.

Pace yourself! Your goal is not to be a hero. It's to do the slow, difficult work of creating justice.

HEALTH CARE

CLIMATE CHANGE

ANIMAL WELFARE

HOW TO
MAKE A
PROTEST SIGN

Protesting is a way of saying *no*. *No* to injustice of all kinds. *No* to racism. *No* to policies or politicians that are hurting people or the planet. If you are going to a protest (it might also be called a demonstration, vigil, or march), you'll want to make a sign to express how you feel and/or what you want to happen.

1 **Brainstorm.** For the most powerful words, check in with how you feel. "Black Lives Matter" is a very expressive message, and so is something in your own words, like "I'm so angry about racism. It needs to end now." Or quote an activist or artist you love.

2 **Get a piece of cardboard of any size.** You can cut it from a shipping or cereal box, or you can repurpose the posterboard from your fourth grade "Camels and Their Humps" report.

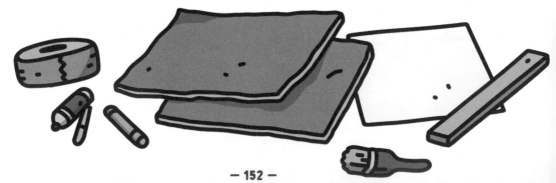

3 **Draft your message in pencil.** This helps you with the spacing so you can be sure you have enough room. (Have you ever started writing a big, glorious *Happy Birthday* on a card, but then you only have room for *Happy* and *Bir* and you're stuck cramming the rest in along the edge? Oh, uh, us either.)

4 **Write it over.** A thick marker is good; paints and a brush are messier but more fun. Add decorations or don't—it might depend a little on the mood of the event.

5 **Go be a joyful activist!** Activism is hard, but it doesn't need to be dreary.

HOW TO
CHANGE THE WORLD

Being the best person you can be is honestly the most powerful tool you have for change. But there are some noisier ones, too:

Talk openly, courageously, and optimistically with your family and friends about what you believe and why.

Use social media to share books, ideas, causes, songs, art, and whatever else you can to spread the word. Share a poem about being gay. List your five favorite Asian American authors. Do an interpretive dance about the benefits of solar energy.

Write to your school administration insisting that they teach a more diverse range of books, adopt a Black Lives Matter curriculum, or start a recycling program.

Contact your political representatives by email or phone to demand that they address the issues you care about. It's okay if you don't have the solutions all figured out. "I'm really worried about the prisons in our state being overcrowded," you can tell your senator. "I'm hoping you will make a plan to address this."

SOLAR ENERGY

Be noisy when you need to be. As congressperson John Lewis once said, "Never, ever be afraid to make some noise and get in good trouble, necessary trouble."

Don't forget to **read the newspaper** (or tap into other reliable news sources) to stay informed about what's going on in the world.

POP QUIZ

There's no recycling bin in your school cafeteria, and everyone just throws all their cans and bottles into the trash. What do you do?

1 Decide not to worry about it. If this planet doesn't work out, we can always move to the moon! #ThatMoonLife

2 Research school recycling programs and see what kind of funding or grants are available for starting one.

3 Send an email to your school's administration about it.

4 Gather your friends and brainstorm ways to raise awareness about climate change.

Answer: 2, 3, and 4! It takes time and energy to make the world better, but it's always worth it.

SPREAD LOVE

If there's one single thing you can do
to make the world a better place, it's this.
Tell people you love them.
Show them your love with your caring actions.

Be a force of kindness in your home, your school,
your friend group, your neighborhood, your town, and the world.
You will never, ever regret it.

A lovingly critical eye is pretty much every writer's dream, and I am living the dream. A few eagle-eyed, big-hearted early readers made this book so much better: Storey's beta reader, Ronni Davis; editor (and former student) Katherine Duke; and my daughter, Birdy Newman. Thank you.

Although the authors likely wouldn't recognize their work in these pages, a few books changed the course of my thinking while I was writing: *Emergent Strategy* by adrienne maree brown; *So You Want to Talk About Race* by Ijeoma Oluo; and *Sitting Pretty* by Rebekah Taussig. I am so grateful to these authors for putting their beauty and brilliance out into the world.

I love Storey so much—including everyone there I've ever had the immense pleasure of working with: the fabulous Deborah Balmuth and Deanna Cook, whose early enthusiasm for this project got (and kept) the ball rolling; Mia Lumsden, who is as graceful, wise, and patient an editor as you could ever hope for; Ash Austin, who brought all her colorful, designer-flair mojo to the pages; Alee Moncy, who is the champion of champions in every way; generous upstander Alethea Morrison; megasuperstar Margaret Lennon; and Maribeth Casey, who gets it done— and so well.

The lovely Jennifer Gates always knows exactly what to do and how best to hold my hand while doing it. And illustrator Debbie Fong continues to embody the absolute dream-team combo of love, hilariousness, and imagination.

I am, as always, so grateful for the years of pleasurable and profound conversations with my friends and family, especially, as always, Michael, Ben, and Birdy, who are always completely gracious and game to talk about anything, including how to talk about stuff. I couldn't love you more—as I believe I have successfully communicated, ha ha ha.

And dear readers, thank you. You make me want to say it all better.

Here's what people are saying about
HOW TO BE A
PERSON

- - - - - - - - - - - - - - - - - - - -

"Kids will delight in this witty, clear, and fun-to-read handbook. And parents will rejoice in having Catherine Newman as a wise and warm partner in teaching our children nearly everything they should know—but don't want to hear about from us!"

— **DR. LISA DAMOUR,** author of *Untangled* and *Under Pressure*

"Catherine Newman has created a starting place for loving, productive conversations about independence, competence, and kindness."

— **JESSICA LAHEY,** author of *The Gift of Failure*

"An illustrated guide that teaches tweens (who aren't eager to learn anything from you) life skills such as managing money, doing the dishes, and addressing an envelope."

— *PARENTS*

"Geared toward kids—but honestly, everyone in the house should brush up on these cleaning and life skills."

— *REAL SIMPLE*

"Emphasizes why these skills are so important for kids to master and how good they'll feel once they do. The illustrations reflect diversity and avoid gender stereotypes. Entertaining way to teach valuable skills that every kid (and adult) needs to know."

— *BOOKLIST*

"This succinct and entertaining guidebook describes life skills with step-by-step instructions. . . . No matter who is reading and enjoying the book, the skills are fleshed out with easy-to-understand steps and engaging illustrations."

— *SCHOOL LIBRARY JOURNAL*